CW00664040

Needle Felting W...
With
Jenny Barnett

*Learn to needle felt using wool fleece and
barbed needles to sculpt the wool into a
wonderful collection of animal characters*

For my Mum and Dad
and my husband
Kevin

This book is a guide on needle felting. The items described are not recommended as toys.

The written instructions, photographs, designs, illustrations and projects in this volume are intended for the personal use of the reader, and may be reproduced for that reason only. Any other use, especially commercial use is forbidden under law without written permission of the copyright holder.
All rights reserved.
No part of this book may be reproduced in any form or by any means, electronic or mechanical, including photocopying, recording, or by any information storage and retrieval system, without permission in writing from the publisher

Every effort has been made to ensure that all the information in this book is accurate. However, due to differing conditions, tools, and individual skills, the publisher cannot be responsible for any injuries, losses, or other damages that may result from the use of this book
All recommendations are made without guarantee on the part of the author or publisher.

Copyright belongs to Jenny Barnett 2014

First published in Great Britain in 2014 by Jenny Barnett Printed in the United Kingdom

Design and text, Illustration and photography Jenny Barnett

Foreword

An apology to all husbands

Foreword by Jenny's husband

I should like to take this opportunity to apologise to all the husbands whose wives have purchased this book. The next few years will be a difficult time for you. Those of you that have not mastered the art of cooking or got to grips with the intricacies of the washing machine will probably fall by the wayside first, as you become abandoned in your droves as your long loving spouses fall under the terrible spell that is needle felting.

Your once clean and respectable home will soon become invaded by hundreds of miniature woodland creatures, whose beady eyes will stare at you from every available shelf, nook or cranny.

Old friends whom you once cherished will no longer call, or will go to great lengths to avoid you in the street, in case they are presented with yet another curious hare, or not so obvious badger.

Some of you will be forced to wear needle felted fox~head tie pins, or suffer the indignity of having small sheep attached to the top of your favourite slippers.

On the plus side I have never lost my set of keys since I have had a six inch chicken dangling from the bunch. I have however lost my garage, which is now a fully functioning needle felting factory supplying Europe with a menagerie of woolly delights.

Finally, when choking on loose fleece that has all too often found its way into the occasional cooked meal, or hurriedly 'thrown together' sandwich, I always think that a trip down to the local, for a couple of hours imbibing on several medicinal pints of your favourite tipple a perfect cure for dislodging wayward fibres.

In the most extreme cases, such as my own, you might find yourself being forced to kiss the latest felty offering.

Be strong my brothers.

K.R.Barnett

Needle felted sheep doll. Poem by K R Barnett.

Silas Sheerbag was a well groomed sheep
Who could knit his own fleece to earn his own keep
People travelled from all over the land
Just to view a sheep with airs so grand
And each visitor to his stately stable
Would leave a gold coin upon his table
Each shiny coin the price of an hours sit
For where else could you watch a well groomed sheep knit.

Contents

also throughout the book, look out for the tip~tags

Introduction

This book is designed to inspire you to take up your felting needles and fibres, and give you the confidence to go on to invent your own wonderful, expressive wool characters. You are in for a treat!

Inside this book you will find plenty of ideas and encouragement to get you started, with hints and tips to help you gain the most enjoyment from this amazing art form.

You are going to be modelling with wool, making simple shapes, joining them together, and with a bit of concentration and practice, transforming them into unique, tactile miniature sculptures.

Working in this way can be similar to other making techniques like clay or dough modelling. The best part of creating your character is the posing - clever positioning of the figure, so it's not just a static pose, you will learn how to add your own twist.

Take your time and enjoy needle felting

Your Needle felted creations improve the more time you spend working on them, so it's not for the impatient... but it is good to slow down and be creative for a while in this fast paced world. The rhythmic, meditative nature of felting can be very calming and therapeutic, very rewarding as you watch the small sculpture take form and evolve at your fingertips.

There is an element of risk involved, as you are using very sharp needles and a jabbing motion, you can pierce your skin, but be careful and be brave! Just relax, and take your time to get used to the needles. Keep your eyes on your work all the time. No matter what your level of experience, if you follow the simple steps, you can needle felt, finding your own rhythm and technique and make something that is unique to you.

Needle felting is not recommended for young children, but older children can be encouraged to explore its possibilities with a little supervision.

The collection of projects in the book may be made by complete beginners, even if you have no experience of modelling or needle felting.

Follow the projects at your own pace, adapt them to suit you. Try not to be concerned with producing an exact copy of the examples, you will naturally develop your own style and your sculptures will be one of a kind, unique to you.

Once you have completed several of these creations, I am sure you will be confident in your abilities to begin your own ideas, possibly a sculpture of your own pet, or favourite animal or bird.

Most importantly, enjoy being creative with the wool.

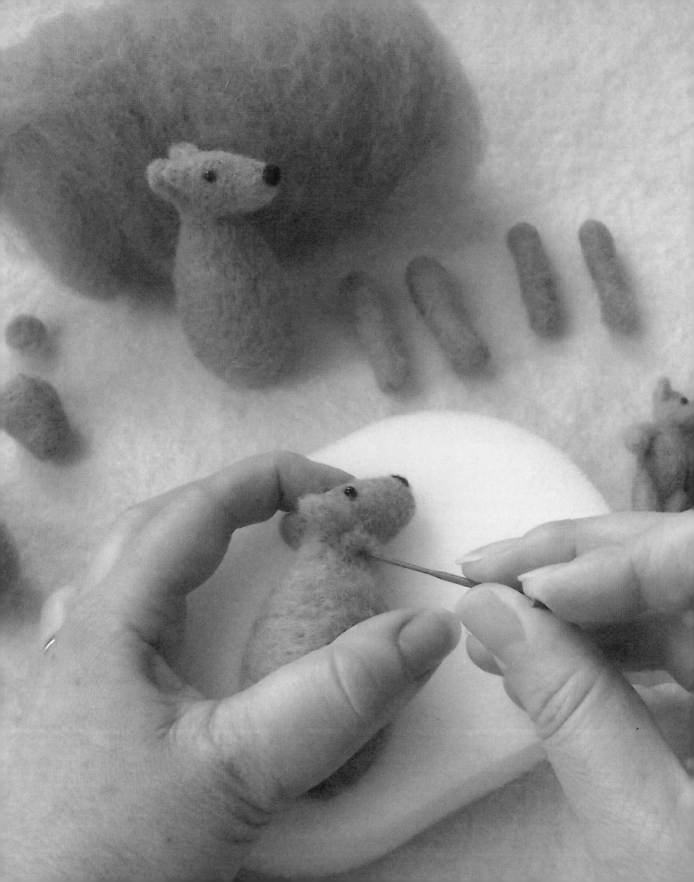

What is Needle Felting ?

Needle felting is the action of repeatedly pushing a sharp, barbed needle into dry wool fleece, to tangle the fibres together, forming a solid flat or three dimensional mass of felt. The barbs on the needle will catch fibres and push them into one another causing them to lock together. The fibres have tiny scales on them which also work to aid the felting process and prevent the fibres from untangling.

The more this action is repeated, the more tangled the fibres become, shrinking and firming up the form, which can then be added to, and moulded into shapes and joined with other forms to create a sculptural object.

You can make any variety of shapes and dimensions depending on the amount of fleece and action and direction of the needles.

If a piece you are needle felting becomes too small, you can simply add more loose fleece to make it grow bigger. Or if a piece is still quite large, but soft, you can continue to needle felt, and the form will shrink as the fibres become more tangled and compacted.

The more 'needling' you do the better, as the shape will shrink in size and become more firm and solid and refined.

Each model is made up of several pieces which are quite simple shapes, joined together. Even a complicated looking sculpture can be achieved by breaking it down into smaller sections and looking at the colours and shapes.

Lumps and bumps can be smoothed out, or covered with more fleece when the model is put together.

In the pictures below, you can see the white wool pulled back to reveal that the fibres have been pushed into the brown wool fleece with the barbed felting needle

Foam Sponge

Wool Fleece

Tissue
Plaster
wet-wipes
hand cream

Felting
needles

Scissors
needle
thread

Sketch book
+ pens

Wooden
skewers

Beads

Wire

Hand Carders
or
Dog grooming brush
x2

Pliers
wire cutters

Things you will need

Materials you will need, and some other items you may find very useful. More details of each are included in the following pages.

Wool fibres ~ natural or dyed wool tops or wool batts

Felting needles ~ 36 gauge triangle and 38 gauge star

Sponge ~ foam sponge or flat brush to support your work

Beads ~ small black beads for eyes

Sewing needle and thread ~ to stitch on the eyes

Wire and pliers ~ to make feet etc.

Hand carders ~ or dog grooming combs for mixing and carding wool

Wooden skewers ~ for making long or very small shapes

Tissues ~ wet-wipes and first aid plasters, just in case you pierce your skin

Sketchbook ~ or notebook for keeping notes on ideas and inspiration

Scissors

Some other useful items, not pictured

Cardboard ~ recycled cardboard helps when making flat shapes

Hot melt glue gun ~ for making the wire unicorn horns, and acorns.

Decoration ~ some ribbons threads and fabric, beads, sequins

11

Felting Needles

actual size

enlarged

Felting needles are made for industrial felting machinery, where thousands of needles work together punching up and down into fibres to make machine~made felt.
They are available to use individually in different 'gauges' with different size 'barbs' on them, so you can choose a needle which works best with your project.

For all the creations in this book you can use both 36 gauge triangle and 38 gauge star
Details of suppliers can be found on page 108

36 gauge triangle
This needle has quite visible barbs on the three edges of the needle.
Ideal for starting a sculpture, it's great for building up and firming the shapes.
Push this needle quite deeply into the wool to felt all the way through the shape.

38 gauge star.
This is finer than the above needle and has smaller barbs on four edges. You will feel the difference straight away, felting will be a little slower, but you have much more control.
This needle is great for joining pieces together, pushed in quite deeply.
It is also perfect for finishing off the surface of your model, with more shallow needling all over, and for adding surface detail like colours and patterns.

Felting needles can snap if you bend, lever or twist them, so try to keep them straight as you push them into the wool. Try not to go too fast especially if there is some wire inside the wool.
Keep some spares handy.

The type of sponge, foam or brush support is optional. There are flat, upturned brushes available, or blocks of car wash, bath sponge, or upholstery foam will do.

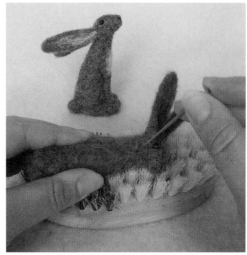

To identify your needles at a glance, paint the blunt end with brightly coloured nail varnish or enamel paint. Colour~code or label them.

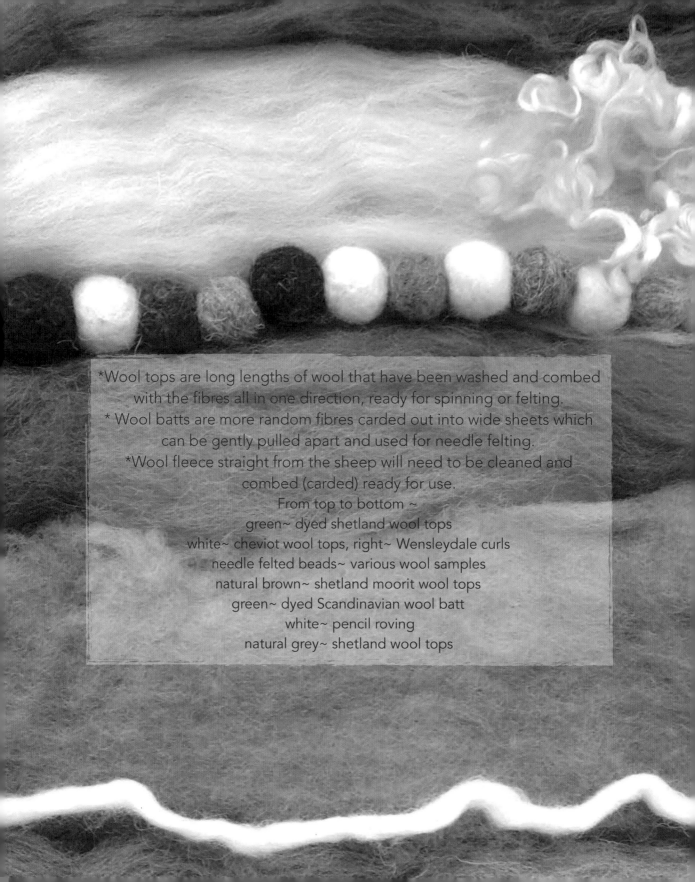

*Wool tops are long lengths of wool that have been washed and combed with the fibres all in one direction, ready for spinning or felting.
* Wool batts are more random fibres carded out into wide sheets which can be gently pulled apart and used for needle felting.
*Wool fleece straight from the sheep will need to be cleaned and combed (carded) ready for use.
From top to bottom ~
green~ dyed shetland wool tops
white~ cheviot wool tops, right~ Wensleydale curls
needle felted beads~ various wool samples
natural brown~ shetland moorit wool tops
green~ dyed Scandinavian wool batt
white~ pencil roving
natural grey~ shetland wool tops

Wool

Wool fleece and animal fibres are available in many colours, natural or dyed.
For the designs in this book, some wool types and the quantities are suggested for you.
Depending on how many models you wish to make you can calculate how much fleece
you will need. Wool batts are ideal, and ready for needle felting. If you have wool tops,
you may wish to card the wool a little first.

Carding (combing) the wool prepares the clean fibres ready for use. You can use small dog~
grooming combs to prepare small amounts, or find larger hand carders from the suppliers on
page 108
You may wish to blend some colours of your own, or create different shades of colour for
surface detail. Just like mixing paint, you can mix quantities of fibre with the combs.
Here's a tip on using the combs, just reverse the instructions if you are left~handed.

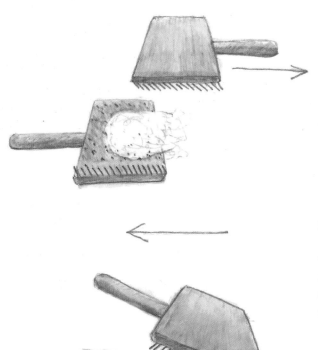

*1 Place some fibres to be mixed onto the
surface of one comb.
Hold in the left hand and rest on your lap.*

*2 Gently comb across the fibres outwards, to
the right with the other comb in your right
hand, several times.*

*3 Lift the fibres from the bottom comb by
turning both handles towards you and
combing the fibres off the lower comb, towards
you, with the higher comb.*

*4 With the handles still towards you, push the
higher comb forwards and onto the lower
comb, this will transfer all the fibre back onto
the lower comb and turn the fibres over.*

*5 Turn the combs back out to the sides again
and repeat step 2 .
Continue with this sequence until you are happy
with the blend.*

ouch!

Starting to Needle Felt

Practice making some of the shapes on the following pages.
Use about 5 grammes fleece, and a 36 gauge triangle needle.
Roll up the fleece on the table and pinch it into a tight bundle.
Push the needle steadily and quite deeply into the wool, repeat several times.
You will feel and hear the barbs of the needle catching the fibres, tangling them together. You can turn over the bundle of fleece and carry on needling all around to create your shape.
Remember the more you needle felt, the more the bundle will shrink. If your shape is still soft, and quite big, keep needling ~ it will get smaller. Alternatively if the bundle becomes too small, you can add more fleece to the surface, making the shape grow.

* Keep your eyes on what you are doing all the time!
* Rest your work on top of the sponge support, you will have a better hold, and are less likely to pierce your skin.
* Keep the needles straight, avoid bending them to prevent snapping

Roll up the fleece tight. The tighter/ firmer you can pinch the fibres together, the less needle felting it will need to firm up.

To demonstrate the shrinkage, these equal amounts of fleece have been needle felted for different amounts of time. From left to right~ 1 minute, 2 minutes, 3 minutes and the smallest was needle felted for over 5 minutes (not to scale)

Making 3D Shapes

All of the models are made up of simple shapes, the following illustrations (not to scale) are a guide to forming them.

When you are making shapes that are going to be joined together, leave a little loose fibre,eg. Leave the neck loose for attaching the head.

The direction you aim the needle is the direction the shape will shrink, so you can change the shape of the bundle depending on the direction you poke the needle.
You can also use your fingers and palms to pinch, pull and roll the bundle, to mould into the desired shape.

Round/ Spherical
Roll and pinch the fleece into a tight round bundle and hold firm on top of the foam pad and needle felt a ball.
Move the ball around and needle felt all directions to create a curved surface.

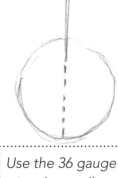

Oval /oblong /egg (eg. sheep/horse/ bear/robin/badger body)
Roll the fleece into a longer cylinder shape, and needle felt along the length, vertically more.
Round off the ends as for the ball shape .
For more of an egg shape, you can add some fibres to one end to make it bigger, or keep needling the other end to make it smaller, or a combination of both.

Use the 36 gauge triangle needle. Push the needle in quite slowly and deeply to felt all the way through, not just the surface. This will help firm up the shape.

18

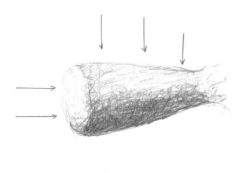

Cone (eg. fox and hare body)
As you roll up the fleece, you can fold one edge over to create a thicker end.
Flatten the wider end by needle felting directly into the end of the length horizontally, to push the fibres in. Be careful not to stab into your fingers.

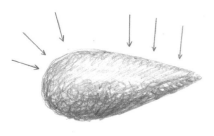

Pear drop (eg. seal body and head, fox head)
Similar to the cone shape, but don't flatten the wide end, just needle gently all around to create the roundness, like the ball, and needle in a line along the length of the pointed end, vertically. Turn it over and repeat, but not directly into the length horizontally as this will make the shape blunt.

Rugby ball (eg. chicken body)
Roll up the bundle, pull out the pointed ends and needle vertically along the length of the shape, turning over and repeating, but not directly into the ends horizontally .
Push the pointed ends up by pinching and pulling into shape with your fingers and directional needling!

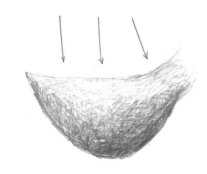

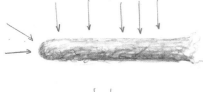

Sausage or log shape (eg. legs and feet or chicken head)
Roll a piece of fleece up as tight as you can and needle felt all along the length , turning over occasionally.
You can also try the wooden skewer technique described on page 21.
Leave one end loose for attaching to the body.
Needle felt the foot end into the desired shape, eg. round for a paw or flat for a hoof.

When making 2 or more of any shape, it's good to have the equal amounts prepared first, so that they will be roughly the same size when made.

Wooden Skewer Technique

Wooden skewer , or bamboo kebab stick technique. This is a great way make sausage shapes for legs, or pointed shapes for beaks and ears, and tiny bobbles for the chicken's wattles and comb.

Wrap and twist the fleece around the wooden skewer. If you need to add a length of wire as support you can wrap this inside the fleece, so it is trapped.

It helps to grip the wool if you moisten the wood with a wet wipe or damp cloth.

First moisten the skewer with a damp cloth or wet-wipe, this helps the fleece to grip. Roll the fleece around the skewer.

Hold on tightly to the fleece and continue to twist the skewer, until you feel the fibres tighten around the stick.

Hold the roll of fleece on top of the sponge and gently remove the skewer.
Needle felt along the length of fleece to prevent unravelling.

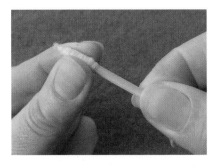

Ears for unicorn & seahorse
Wrap a small amount of fleece around the point of the skewer. Pinch and hold tight whilst twisting the skewer until the fibres tighten, and a point is made at the tip. Remove, hold tight and needle felt a little to stop it unravelling.

Beaks for robin and chicken
Experiment making the same way as for ears on the left.
Or try wet~felting the beaks, making two at a time, see page 24

Wattles and comb for chicken
Try using the point of a cocktail stick.
Wrap a tiny wisp of fleece around the very tip of the point of the skewer. Hold tight and twist to create a bobble of wool. Pinch and remove the bobble and needle felt into position.

21

Making Flat Shapes

Flat shapes like ears and wings can be made by needle felting the fleece down on top of the sponge.

Practice with a small amount of fleece and use the 36 gauge triangle needle.

Place the fleece on the sponge and needle felt with shallow jabs all across the surface.

The fibres will attach to the foam, so peel the fleece from the surface and turn over and needle felt the other side, repeat this until the wool becomes a flat piece of felt.

*You may find the fibres show through the other side... So use the finer 38 gauge star needle and lower the angle to horizontal, so that the fibres go into the felt.

Create a nice crisp edge to your flat shape, and protect your fingers with this simple tip using some recycled cardboard packaging.
Use the finer 38 gauge star needle to push in the loose fibres around the edge of your shape.

  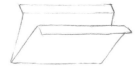

Cut a piece of card about 10 x 15 cm Fold in half.

Fold back the 2 long edges about 2 cm.

Hold the felt inside the card and gently needle felt into the edges.

Hold the flat piece of felt in place, inside the card.
With the 38 gauge star needle, gently push the stray fibres into the gap.
Needle felt all along the edge, then turn the piece around and repeat.
Remove the flat piece to check the shape, and adjust if necessary.

```
If a flat shape becomes a little
short  or thick, pinch both ends
and pull ( wiggle the ends from
side to side a little whilst
pulling) to stretch the piece
longer.
The opposite can be done to make
a piece wider.
This can help to match up a
pair.
```

Making beaks and legs

Here's how to make the beaks and wire legs for the **chicken** and **robin**, and the **unicorn** horn. For wire suppliers see page 108

This is a quick way of wet~felting two beaks at once.

1 Roll up a small amount of fleece in a ball, and dip this into some soapy water. Gently roll it in circles between your palms until it starts to felt into a ball.

2 Using more pressure roll your palms in a forwards and backwards motion to squash the ball lengthways .

3 Continue to roll until the shape is firmly felted and pointed at both ends. About 3 cms long is a good size.

4 Rinse out the soap and leave to dry, then cut in half to create two beaks.

*To make a horn for the **Unicorn,** wrap half of a 5cm length of wire with thread, ribbon or string, depending on the effect you like. A tiny blob of glue from a hot glue gun at each end will help as you start and finish the binding. Make a loop at the base of the horn to be trapped in the fibre to hold secure.

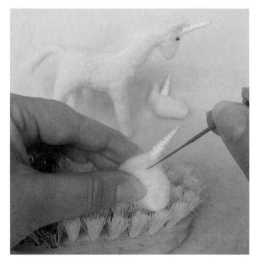

Bend the end of the wire into a loop. This will be trapped inside the wool and hold the horn in place when you needle felt the head.

Gardening wire or jewellery/ florist wire can be use to make effective little legs for **robins** and **chickens**. You can even bind the wire with thread for a quite lifelike effect.
Experiment and make a selection of different sizes and lengths to choose from to suit your model.
Beware, cutting the wire will create sharp edges, use a file to make them blunt if necessary.
(The drawings below are not to scale)

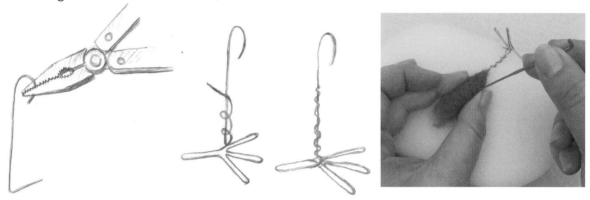

Chicken legs. *Use the wire straight from the coil or spool. Start at the top by bending around a loop (this will be hidden and trapped inside some fleece to stop the leg falling out). Leave a straight length about 5 cms from the top of the loop, then bend at a right~angle to begin creating the toes. Fold the wire back on itself for the first toe, about 2cms, then bend out again from the base for the next toe, and repeat until you have made four toes. Adjust the position so there are three at the front, one at the back. Twist some wire up around the leg, then cut at the base of the loop.*

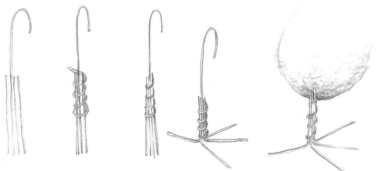

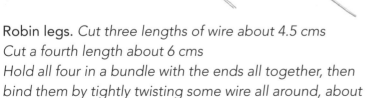

Robin legs. *Cut three lengths of wire about 4.5 cms*
Cut a fourth length about 6 cms
Hold all four in a bundle with the ends all together, then bind them by tightly twisting some wire all around, about half way up the shorter lengths.
Cut the wire at the top of the shorter lengths.
Bend the longer length into loop. This will be covered and trapped with fleece to hold the legs in place.

```
* resist the
temptation to open out
the toes until the
robin is complete, as
the toes will get in
your way and cover you
in scratches!
```

25

Posing your character

This is the fun part, you are in control of how your model looks and you really can give it some character, and attitude when you join the pieces together and add more detail.
As the model develops you will find you can influence how it looks depending on the combination of positions you put the eyes, ears and head and limbs.

It helps to think a little about body language, and gesture. Try making some sketches.
Play around with the positioning of the eyes on the head, the angle of the ears and the direction of the gaze. You can even needle felt a little smile.

If in doubt, try tilting the head up so your model is looking upwards from the worktop and gazing back at you. Here are some examples for the hare.

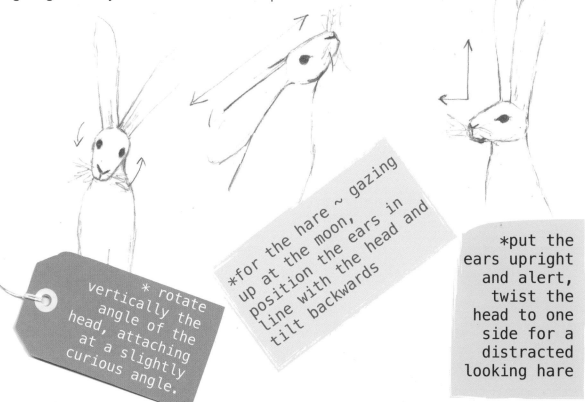

* rotate vertically the angle of the head, attaching at a slightly curious angle.

*for the hare ~ gazing up at the moon, position the ears in line with the head and tilt backwards

*put the ears upright and alert, twist the head to one side for a distracted looking hare

Joining pieces together

Join sections of the model together by needle felting the loose fibres from one piece to the other .

Further secure the connection by adding some more fleece over the join and felting into both sections.

It is easier to use the finer 38 gauge star needle to join sections together because now your felt has firmed up, the 36 gauge triangle is difficult to push into the wool.

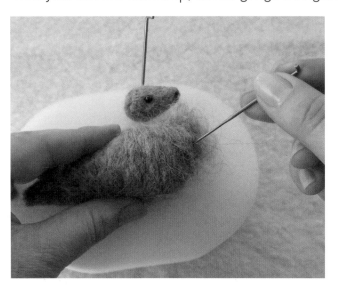

Head onto body
If there are no loose fibres to felt together, just add some spare to one of the pieces by needle felting some deeply into the surface

Remember to try different angles and positions of the pieces,to create the pose and character

Ears onto head.
Support the felt on the foam or you will surely stab into your fingers.

Hold everything in place and push the needle through the loose fibres at the base of the ear, pushing them right through and into the head. You can add a wisp of fibre over the join and needle felt this into place to really secure the ear.

Use this same technique for attaching wings and tails onto chickens and robins.

28

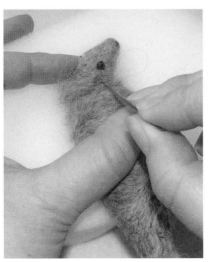
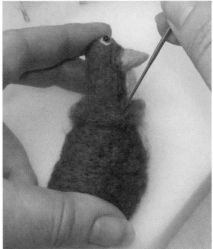

Head onto body

Hold the pieces firmly on top of the foam and needle felt the loose fibres from one section into the other.

Turn the model over to the other side and needle felt some more. Turn the model again and continue all around the join. Place some more fleece over the join and needle felt into place and build up the neck if needed

Legs onto body

For the hare and the fox pose, you can needle felt the legs onto the body just at the edge of the shape and all along the very edge of the length. Keep needling the top of the leg to blend in with the chest, which can be built up with more fleece.

The overhang at the bottom can be folded upwards to create the paw.

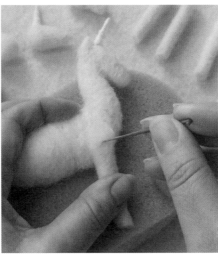

Legs onto body-standing pose

Needle felt the loose fibres at the top of the leg into the body, and then cover the join with some more fleece over the surface to secure.

Adding some more fleece underneath the join will prevent the legs from wobbling.

29

Sewing on the Eyes

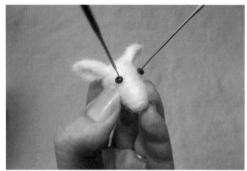

Bring your character alive by adding shiny black beads for eyes.

Follow the guides on the following pages for the different characters.

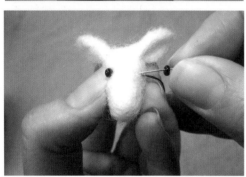

*use your felting needles as pins to position the beads onto the face, and see the different effects you can create, just by moving them around a little.

From left to right...
Wide apart at the sides looks quite natural
Close together can look more cartoon~like
Further down the face creates a younger look.

right~different styles can also be achieved ,
depending on the shape that you make the head.

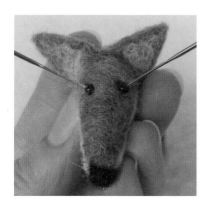

When you are ready to sew the eyes in place, use a double thread, knot the end and sew up under the neck, the knot will be hidden when the head is attached to the body.

Knot the end of your double thread.
Sew the first stitch from underneath the head at the neck area and sew out through to the position of the first eye.

Push the needle through the hole in the bead and sew back through from the first eye to the position of the second eye. Pull the thread tight to position the bead.

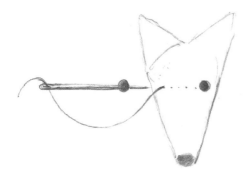

Place the second bead onto the needle and sew back into the head from the position of the second eye back to the first. Sew out to just behind the bead.

Repeat the stitches to secure the eyes.

To finish, push the needle behind the bead and sew back out to the base of the head at the neck and make a couple of small stitches to secure the thread and cut.

Stitching Noses

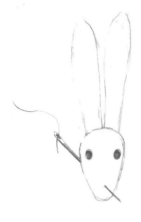

For the nose of the hare and the sheep you can stitch the letter **Y**. You can over~stitch the lines to make the nose more visible.

Sew back from beneath the head through to the centre front of the face .

Make a diagonal stitch above to create one half of the letter **V**. Sew back towards the centre.

Repeat the diagonal stitch on the opposite side to complete the letter V. Sew back to the centre.

Sew a vertical stitch below the **V** to create the stem of the **Y**. Sew back to the centre.
Repeat the stitches to make the nose more visible if necessary.

Sew the thread back under the head to the knot and make a couple of stitches to secure the thread, then cut.

For the nose of the grey seal you can stitch two dark nostrils.

33

Finishing Touches

Needle felting the surface.

When your model is all put together, continue needle felting. Use the finer 38 gauge star needle. The more you work on it, the more it will improve. It will become more solid and have a smoother surface.

If you have any lumpy areas or creases, just cover the area with some more fibres and felt over the surface.

You can achieve different surface effects by adding various types of fleece for colour and texture.

Apply fibres to the surface just like painting, creating shading or patterns.

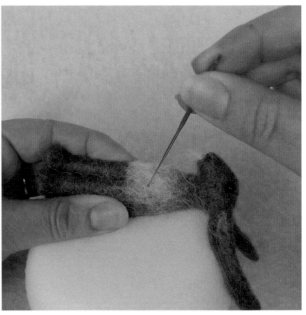

When adding some white fibre for the furry chest of fox or hare, add tiny wisps at a time. Put too much on and the patch becomes more of a blob.

Adding Whiskers...
Add some fabulous whiskers to your hare, or seal using a coarse fibre like masham or herdwick or even horse hair or goat hair.

 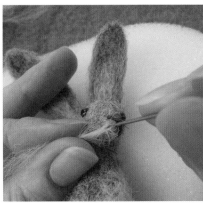 

Take a tiny pinch of the fibre and fold in half , to form a loop and hold tight.
Use the finer 38 gauge needle as the 36 will be hard to push in, and can snap.

Position the fold to one side of the nose and carefully push some fibres deep into the nose with the felting needle. Repeat with some more fibres if needed. Add some whiskers to the other side of the nose in the same way.

Tease out any loose fibres and trim with scissors, or just leave long and wild looking.

The Workshops

Here is the collection of characters for you to create, there are also some smaller, extra items you can make to complement each sculpture. With each workshop there is a guide to the fibres to try, and the approximate time they may take, but work at your own pace and remember, the longer you needle felt them, the better they look. Enjoy!

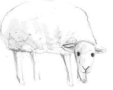

Sheep

Standing sheep made with Jacob fleece, about 8cm tall.
Make the sheep up with simple shapes, then add as much fleece
as you like to create a woolly coat.
Create a small flock of various shapes and sizes. Swap the
colour of fleece for a black sheep, or make the head and legs in
a darker fleece, with a white coat. Look at the many different
breeds for ideas. Add some curled horns for a ram.

Sheep

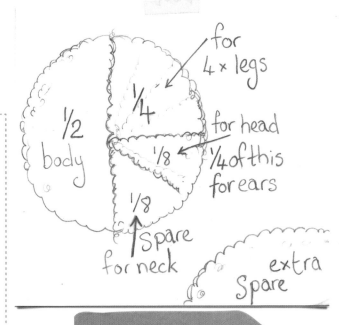

for 4 x legs

for head

1/4 of this for ears

1/2 body

1/4

1/8

1/8

Spare for neck

extra Spare

Materials you will need

10 grammes white wool fleece. Plus some extra spare.
Wire - for inside the legs for support (optional)
4 x lengths about 3cm
2 small black 3mm beads for eyes

Size will be about 8 - 10cm
Time to needle felt 2- 3 hours

SHEEP ~ 10 gms
Try~ Corriedale
Shetland, Jacob,
Cheviot
Devon, Suffolk

1 Body.
Use the 36 gauge triangle needle.
Split the 10 grammes of fleece in two, and put half aside for making the head and legs later...
Roll the other half of fleece tightly into a bundle and hold firmly on top of the sponge. Push the felting needle deeply into the bundle and repeat, until it holds together without springing back open. Turn the wool bundle over and continue to needle felt all around. Aim for about the size and shape on the left.

Leave one end slightly loose for attaching a head and neck. Needle felt all around the other end to make it nice and rounded. Later you can add more fleece to make more of a woolly coat.

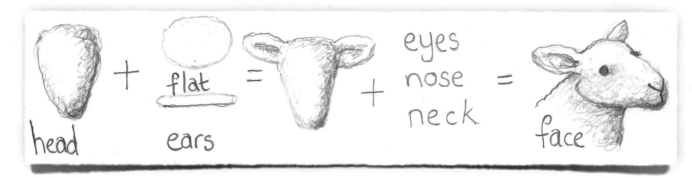

head + flat ears = + eyes nose neck = face

2. Head. *Use the finer 38 gauge star needle.*
Split the remainder of fleece put aside in two, and put half aside for the legs.
Split the remainder in two again, putting half aside for the neck and tail.
What you have left should be just right for the head, including the ears, so take away about one quarter for the two ears.
Roll up the remainder into a smaller, tight bundle to create an oval shape. Try it for size against the body, if it seems a bit big, take some fleece away. If too small, add some fleece from the spare.
Needle felt all around the head until firm. Aim for about the size and shape above left.

3. Ears. *Use the finer 38 gauge star needle, this will be quite fiddly!*
Take the fleece put aside for the ears and split in two. One at a time, roll up in your palms into a loose ball, then needle felt each piece flat on top of the sponge, peel off, turn over and needle felt to flatten the other side. Needle felt the outside fibres towards the centre and shape into an oval. Leave some loose fibres at the base for joining the ears to the head.
Fold the shapes in half and needle felt the fold to create the hollow of the ears.
Try them for size and position against the head you have made. If they seem too big, simply make two more ears from the spare, using less fleece for each. If too small, add some more fibre.
Attach them by slowly pushing some fibres from the base of the ear deep into the head.

4. Eyes. *Use the felting needles to pin the two beads to the head and find the best position.*
Sew the eyes in place by following the guide on page 30

5. Nose. *Sew a few stitches into the letter Y to create the nose, follow the guide on page 32*

6. Join the head to the body. *Use either needle, and some of the spare fleece. Needle felt some fleece into the body to form a short neck for joining the head.*
Position the head onto the neck, hold in place firmly on top of the foam pad, and needle felt the loose fibres from the neck of the body into the back of the head, and some under the chin. Be careful not to stab through into your fingers!
Turn the model over and repeat all the way around. Add some more spare fleece to build up the neck and help to secure the head to the body.
Keep needling to firm up and shape the neck, check the angle the head is facing and adjust if necessary, and needle felt this firmly so it holds the position.

7. Legs. *Use the 38 gauge star needle.*

Use the fleece put aside for the legs and split into four. The short lengths of wire are going to be trapped inside, so use the finer 38 gauge needle and avoid hitting the wire if you can. Follow the steps below, or try the wooden skewer technique on page 21.

One at a time, place the wire on top of the fleece, and roll each piece up tight into a sausage shape. Needle felt along the length, all around until firm.

Leave the top end loose for attaching to the body.

Aim for about the size and length on the right.

The cloven hoof can be made with a small stitch of dark thread.

One at a time, position each leg against the body, and needle felt the top of each leg into the body.

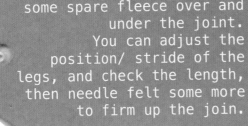

Secure the legs by adding some spare fleece over and under the joint. You can adjust the position/ stride of the legs, and check the length, then needle felt some more to firm up the join.

Finishing touches...

Roll up a small amount of fleece for a tail and needle felt into a short sausage shape, loose at one end, then attach to the sheep's body.

Keep needle felting all over the model to refine the shape and firm up the sheep.

Add as much fleece as you like to create the sheep's woolly coat.

You can even create a curly coat by adding fibres like Wensleydale or Teeswater curls to the

Make a companion, lying down, or make a lamb to go with your sheep.
Use a little less fleece to make it smaller, and bigger beads for the eyes.
Flatten the bottom off to make it stable.

Chicken

Chicken and eggs made with Jacob fleece, about 10 cm
Make these as colourful as you like, or choose a more
natural fleece to look more realistic.
This is a fun creature to make, look at the behaviour of
chickens as they scratch around with their feet and you
will get some ideas for posing them with attitude.
Try using florist wire, or bind the toes and legs with
thread for a really life-like, wrinkly texture.

Chicken

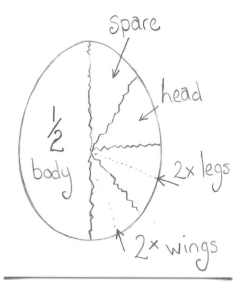

Materials you will need

8 grammes wool fleece in a colour of your choice, plus a little spare
A little red and white fleece for details
Yellow fleece for beak, see page 21 or 24
Wire chicken legs see page 25
2 small black 3mm beads for eyes

Size will be about 8 - 10cm
Time to needle felt 2 to 3 hours

CHICKEN~ 8gms
Try natural~ shetland
or Jacob or cheviot
Try dyed~ Norwegian
or shetland or
Corriedale

1 Body.

Use the 36 gauge triangle needle.
Split the 8 grammes of fleece in two, and put half aside for making the head, legs and wings later...
Roll the other half of fleece tightly into a bundle and hold firmly on top of the sponge. Push the felting needle deeply into the bundle until it holds together without springing back open. Turn the bundle over and needle felt all around.
Pinch and pull some fibres out from one end, needle felt into a point to form the tail.
Leave the neck end slightly loose for attaching the head. Aim roughly for the shape and size on the left.
You can add a little of the spare fleece to adjust the shape if needed.

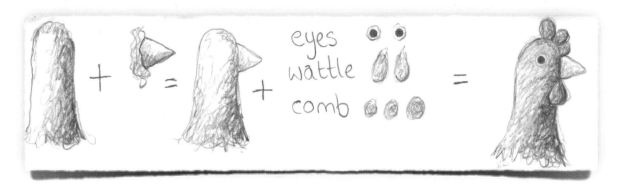

2 Head. *Use the 38 gauge star needle, this will be fiddly.*
Take the other half of fleece put aside, and split in two. Place half aside for the legs and wings.
Split the remainder in two again, half is spare. The remaining amount should be just right for the head of the chicken so roll this up tight to make a sausage shape.
Try this for size against the body, if it seems too big, take a bit of fleece away. For a tip, try the bamboo technique on page 21. Needle felt along the length of the shape, leaving one end loose for attaching to the body.
Needle felt the other end nice and round to form the head.

3. Beak
To make the beak you can follow the instructions on page 24, or use a bamboo skewer technique, see page 21.
Using the finer 38 gauge star needle, position the beak against the head and push the needle in quite deeply all around the edge, catching some fibres from the beak and pushing them into the head.
You will need to add several small wisps of spare fibre over the join, all the way around, and needle felt these thought the edge of the beak and into the head to secure the beak in position.

4. Eyes
Use the felting needles to pin the beads into a position you like on the head.
Knot a double thread and sew into the position of one eye and through to the other side.
Attach the first bead and sew back through in the other direction to the original stitch.

Attach the second bead and stitch right through the head again. You can repeat the stitches to make the eyes secure, then cut the thread close to the surface.
Using the finer needle, place a tiny wisp of white or contrasting fibre over the bead, and gently push the needle deeply in, all around the edge of each bead to create a highlight.

47

5. Join the head to the body. *Use the fine 38 gauge star needle.*
Position the head onto the body, try a curious angle, or turn the head to the left or right, position upright or downwards, pecking the ground perhaps.
When you are ready, hold the head onto the body on top of the sponge, and needle felt some fibres from the neck into the body.
Turn the model over and repeat all around the join until secure. Add some fleece over the join to build up the neck if needed and needle felt to secure the head in position.

6. Wattles and comb.
Your chicken may resemble a pigeon or dove at this stage, so add some 'bobbles' for the wattles and comb.
You can make these in two ways...
Roll up in your fingers and palms five or six tiny amounts of red fibre, or wrap the tiny bits of fibre around the very tip of a cocktail stick and twist them into tight little bundles. See page 21.
Carefully attach to the head with the finer 38 gauge star needle.
Try three or four in a row above the beak, and two below the beak, now it will definitely resemble a chicken.

7. Chicken legs. *Use the fine 38 gauge star needle.*
Split the remaining fleece put aside in two. Put half aside for the wings, and split the remainder in half again for the two legs.
One at a time, wrap the piece of fleece around the wire loop of each leg and carefully needle felt all around and through to make little chicken drumsticks. Be careful not to hit the wire loop too hard, or the needle can snap.

8. Join the legs to the body. *Use either needle.*
Hold the legs against the body, try different positions, e.g. one in front of the other for walking, or pivot the body forward so the hen is tilted down, pecking.
When you like how it looks, one at a time, hold the model on its side on top of the sponge, hold the leg in position and carefully push the needle deep through the thigh and into the body.
Needle felt slowly to prevent catching the wire loop.
You can add some fine fibres over the top, and underneath the legs to firm up the join and prevent the legs from wobbling.

9. Wings. *Use either needle.*

With the remaining fleece put aside, split this in two for the wings (these are optional, the chicken looks quite good without wings).
One at a time, needle felt each piece of fleece flat onto the sponge. Peel from the surface, turn over and repeat until the wool flattens more, then you can needle the edges inwards to shape the wings. See page 23 for some tips on shaping.
Leave the edge to be joined to the body a little loose.
Position each wing against the body, trying different positions for attitude. One at a time needle felt the wings to the body.

Finishing touches.

Now you can 'finesse' your chicken.
Take some tufts of fleece and add these below the tail, behind the legs for shape, and some at the front to build up the chest.
Continue to needle felt all over to create a smooth surface.

Make a little clutch of colourful eggs for your broody hen.
Make a few adjustments like enlarge the comb, add some fancy tail-feathers and make your hen into a cockerel.

49

Bear

Traditional style jointed bear made with dyed shetland fleece, about 8 to 9 cm sitting. Made with simple shapes, the limbs are stitched on so that they are movable for sitting or standing. Enjoy adding a little costume and buttons.
Create your own character or another animal with adjustments to the ears and head for a rabbit or mouse, or add a trunk for an elephant.

Bear

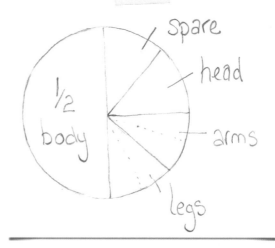

Materials you will need

10 grammes wool fleece. Colour of your choice plus some spare.
Some black fleece for the nose.
White or coloured fleece for decoration.
2 small black 3mm beads for eyes
Matching coloured thread for attaching legs and arms

Size will be about 8 - 10cm
Time to needle felt 2- 3 hours

BEAR~ 10gms
Try~ natural shetland,
cheviot, Jacob,
Dyed~ shetland,
Norwegian/Scandinavian
or Corriedale

1 Body.
Use the 36 gauge triangle needle.
Split the 10 grammes of fleece in two, and put half aside for making the head and legs later...
Roll the other half of fleece tightly into a bundle and hold firmly on top of the sponge.
Push the felting needle deeply into the bundle and repeat until it holds together without springing back open. Turn the bundle over and needle felt all around.
Aim roughly for the shape and size on the left.
Leave the neck end slightly loose for attaching the head.
Needle felt all around the bottom end to make it nice and rounded.
Later you can add more fleece to make it more plump.

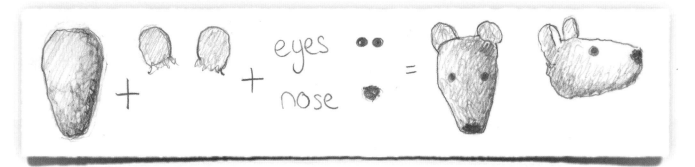

2. Head. *Use the 38 gauge needle*

Take the other half of fleece, split in two and put half aside for the arms and legs.
Split the remainder in two again and put half aside for ears and spare.
The remaining fleece should be just the right amount to make the head, so roll it up as tight as you can and check it for size against the body you have made. If it looks too big, just take a bit of fleece away, if too small, add some fleece from the spare.

3. Ears. *Use either needle.*

Take a small amount of the spare fleece and split into two tufts to make the ears. Roll each loosely into a ball and try for size against the head. Adjust the amount of fleece if necessary. One at a time, needle felt them flat onto the sponge, peel off, turn over and felt the other side.
Needle felt the edges into the small round ear shape with the finer 38 gauge needle.
Leave the edge at the base loose for attaching to the head.
Position as you like at the back of the head and needle felt the loose fibres deep into the head to secure them.

4. Nose. *Use the finer 38 needle and some black fleece.*

Roll a very small amount of fleece into a bobble with your finger tips, and needle felt this into the tip of the nose.

5. Eyes.

Use the felting needles to pin the beads onto the head, and find the best position.
When you like the look, sew the beads in place. See instructions on page 31

6. Join the head onto the body.

Add some spare fleece to the the top of the body to form a loose neck.
Try different positions of the head on the body, then hold in place on top of the sponge.
Using the finer 38 gauge needle, felt some fibres from the neck into the head.
Turn the model over and needle felt all around to secure the head.
Add more spare fleece over the join if needed.

7. Arms and legs. *Use either needle.*
For a short-cut, try the wooden skewer technique on page 21.
Take the fleece put aside for the arms and legs and split into four.
One at a time, roll up into a sausage shape. Try them for size against the bear , and adjust the amount of fleece if necessary. Needle felt all along the length.
You can shape the tips into paws and feet at one end and nice and rounded at the other.

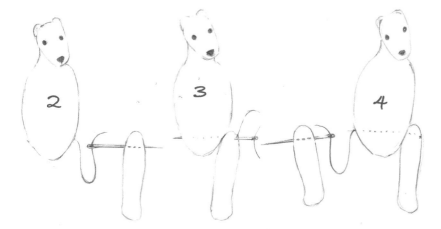

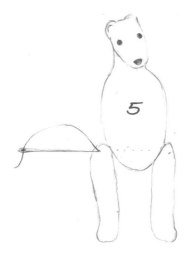

8. Attaching the legs. *Use a longer sewing needle if you have one. Using a matching, double thread , knot the end and sew the limbs onto the body for a jointed, posable bear.*
1.Stitch from one hip to the other.
2. Sew through the centre at the top of one leg, pull thread through.
3. Stitch back through the centre at the top and then sew straight through the hip to the other side.
4. Sew through the centre top of the second leg.
5. Sew back through the centre-top of the second leg and continue the stitch straight through the hips to the first leg. Repeat the stitches again, and secure the thread with a few small stitches under the joint, cut the thread.

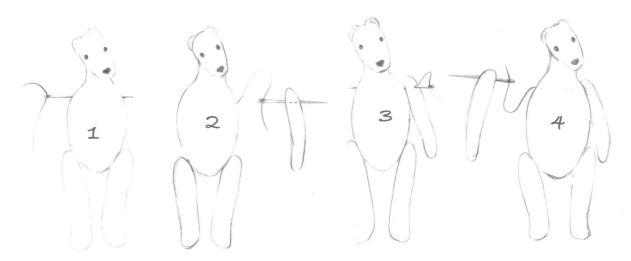

Attaching the arms.

First check the position you would like to attach the arms, by pinning them into the body at the point the shoulders will pivot.

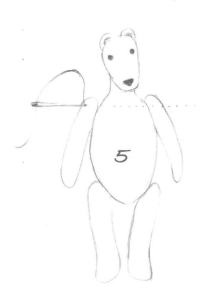

1. *Sew through the shoulders from one side to the other. Pull the thread through.*
2. *Sew through the centre of the top of one arm.*
3. *Sew back through the centre~top of the arm and take the stitch right through the shoulder, out to the other. Pull the thread through.*
4. *Sew through the centre~top of the second arm.*
5. *Sew back through the centre~top of the second arm, stitch straight through the shoulders and out the other side in a straight line. Repeat and finish the same as the legs.*

To make the bear sit on his bottom, without toppling over, make sure to position the hips not too low on the body

Have fun adding costumes and a selection of playthings for your little bears.

To make a little tutu for your bear
Cut a strip of fabric or ribbon about 50 to 60 cms long.
Sew a running stitch along one edge.
Pull the thread along to gather the ribbon.
Stitch onto the bear all around the waist.

Grey Seal

Little Atlantic grey seal made with grey shetland fleece about 13 to 14cm long .
Made quite simply with two pear~drop shapes for the body and head, and four
wedge shapes made into tail and flippers. Take some time to experiment with
how you position these pieces, there are many ways you can pose him, eg. on his
side, sleeping, on his back, or front. Have a look at pictures of groups in their
many shapes and sizes.

Grey Seal

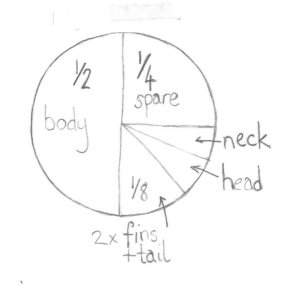

Materials you will need

15 grammes grey wool fleece, plus a little spare

Some lighter and darker shades for details

2 small black 4mm beads for eyes

Whiskers- white masham or grey herdwick fibre

Size will be about 8 - 10cm

Time to needle felt 2- 3 hours

SEAL~ 15gms
Try~ grey
shetland,
cheviot,
Jacob,

1 Body.

Use the 36 gauge triangle needle.

Split the 15 grammes of fleece in two, and put half aside for making the head and flippers later...

Roll the other half of fleece tightly into a bundle and hold firmly on top of the sponge.

Push the felting needle deeply into the bundle and repeat until it holds together without springing back open. Turn the bundle over and continue to needle felt all around. Pinch and pull the fleece out at one end and needle felt along the length to create the point.

Aim roughly for the shape and size on the left.

Needle felt all around the thicker end to make it nice and rounded.

Later you can add more fleece to plump up the seal.

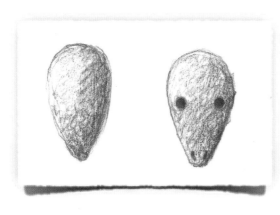

2. Head. *Use either needle*
Take the fleece put aside and split in two, put half aside for the flippers.
Split the remainder in two again and put half aside for the neck and some spare.
The remaining fleece should be just the right amount to make the head, so roll it up as tight as you can and check for size against the body you have made. If it looks too big, just take a bit of fleece away. If too small, add some from the spare.
Needle felt the head into the oval shape, slightly smaller and pointed at one end for the nose.

3. Eyes.
Use the felting needles to pin the beads onto the head and find the best position.
Sew the beads in place following the guide on page 30.

4. Nose.
The nose is created with a couple of diagonal stitches made at the tip.
Sew out to the tip of the nose and make a diagonal stitch to one side, leave a small gap, then make another stitch the other side. See more details on page 33.
The whiskers are best applied as a finishing touch, as they can become crushed.

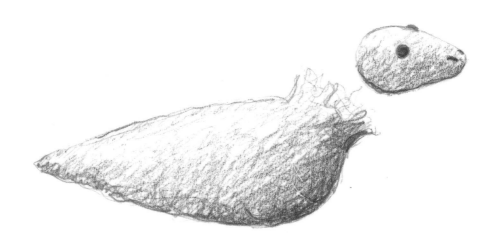

5. Join the head to the body.
First think about how you would like to pose your seal, such as lying on it's back, or side or belly, and try different positions for the head.
Using either needle, and some of the spare fleece, needle felt some tufts of fleece into the body to form a thick neck for securing the head.

5. Join the head to the body... continued. *Use the finer, 38 gauge needle.*
Position the head onto the body, hold in place firmly on top of the foam pad, and needle felt the loose fibres from the neck into the head.
Be careful not to stab through into your fingers!
Turn the model over and repeat all the way around. Add some more spare fleece to build up the thick neck and help to secure the head to the body.
Check the position of the head, adjust if needed, and continue to needle felt until it is firm and fixed in position.

6. Tail and flippers. *Use either needle.*
With the fleece put aside for flippers and tail, split this into four. Roll one piece up tight into a wedge shape, and try it for size against the body. Adjust the amount of fleece if necessary. One at a time, needle felt each flat onto the sponge. Peel from the surface, turn over and repeat until the wool flattens more, then you can needle inwards along the edges to form a wedge shape. See page 23 for some tips on shaping.
Leave the edge to be joined to the body a little loose.
Position two of these at the pointed end of the body, to form a tail. One at a time, needle felt them into the end, then add a little more fleece over the join if necessary.
Try different positions for the flippers, then one at a time, needle felt them into place. Add more fleece over and under the join to secure them.

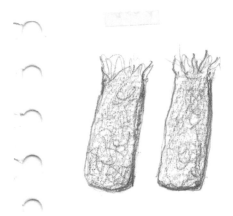

7. Whiskers. *Use the fine 38 gauge needle and some coarse fibre like masham or herdwick.*
Pinch a tiny wisp of coarse fibre and fold over, in half.
Hold the folded loop just over one side of the nose and slowly push some fibres deep into the nose with the needle. Repeat the other side and trim with scissors to a length you like.
See more images on page 35

Finishing touches...
Use the fine 38 gauge star needle.
Add some lighter or darker fibres to create the speckled pattern.
Take tiny wisps and roll up in your fingers and palms into small bobbles, then position at random and needle felt into the surface until smooth.

Create a group of curious seals, just popping their heads out of the water. Make the heads first, then add some fleece for the neck and flatten off the base.

Fox

Fox made with Norwegian pels. Height about 9 cms
This model is made with separate pieces attached to a
cone ~ shaped body.
You can make a running fox by making all four legs
the longer length, with some wire inside for support.
Take a look at the badger, unicorn or sheep
instructions as a guide to positioning them.

Fox

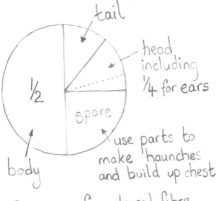

tail

head including ¼ for ears

½

spare

body

use parts to make haunches and build up chest

10 grammes fox coloured fibre

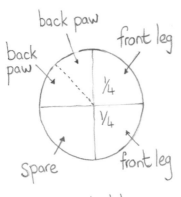

back paw

front leg

back paw

¼

¼

Spare

front leg

3 grammes dark brown

Materials you will need

10 grammes fox coloured wool fleece, plus some spare.
3 grammes dark brown/black fleece
White fleece for details
2 small black 3mm beads for eyes

Size will be about 8 - 10cm
Time to needle felt 3 to 4hours

FOX 10 gms dyed fleece
Try~ Shetland,or
Norwegian pels, or
Corriedale

3 gms dark fleece for
socks
Try black Jacob or Masham

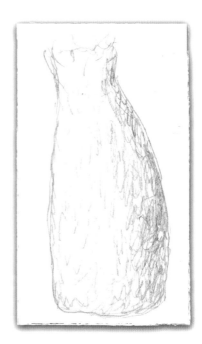

1 Body.
Use the 36 gauge triangle needle.
Split the 10 grammes of fleece in two, and put half aside for making the head and tail later...
Roll the other half of fleece tightly into an oblong shaped bundle (slightly thicker at one end) and hold firmly on top of the sponge.
Push the felting needle deeply into the bundle and repeat until it holds together without springing back open. Turn the bundle over at intervals and continue to needle felt all around.
Aim roughly for the shape and size on the left.
Leave the neck end slightly loose for attaching the head.
Needle felt directly into the bottom end to make it nice and flat.
Later you can add more spare fibre to plump up the fox.

2. Head. *Use the finer 38 gauge needle.*
Split the remaining half of fox fleece and put half aside for spare.
Split the remainder in two again, putting half aside for the tail.
The remaining amount should be just right for the head, including the ears, so take away about a quarter for the two ears.
Roll up the remainder into a smaller, tight bundle. Try for size against the body, and adjust the amount of fleece if necessary. Needle felt to create a pointed cone shape about the size and shape above left. Pinch and pull out the nose a little, needle felt all along the length, turn over and repeat to create the point. Needle felt all around the back of the head until firm.

3. Nose. *Use the finer 38 gauge needle.*
Roll up a small amount of black fleece into a ball in your fingers and needle felt this into the tip of the nose.

4. Ears. *Use either needle. This will be quite fiddly!*
Take the fleece put aside for the ears and split in two. One at a time, roll each piece in your fingers and palms into a loose ball, then needle felt, flat on top of the sponge, peel off, turn over and needle felt to flatten the other side. Needle felt the edges to create the triangle, but leave one edge loose for joining to the head, see tips on shaping on page 23.
Try them for size by positioning against the back of the head you have made. If they seem too big, simply make 2 more ears from the spare, using less fibre for each. If small, add some more fleece.
Attach them by slowly pushing some fibres from the base of the ear deep into the head with the finer 38 gauge needle.
You can add a fine layer of white fibre onto the ears at this stage, or do add this later.

5. Eyes. *Use the felting needles to pin the beads to the head and find the best position.*
Sew the eyes in position by following the guide on page 31.
Add some wisps of white fleece to each side of the face with the fine (38 gauge) needle to create fine - furry cheeks.

6. Join the head to the body. *Use the finer, 38 gauge needle.*

Position the head onto the body, try different positions to create a pose. Hold in place firmly on top of the sponge and needle felt the loose fibres from the neck into head. Be careful not to stab through into your fingers!

Turn the model over and repeat all the way around. Add some more fleece to build up the neck and help to secure the head to the body.

Check the angle the head is facing and adjust if needed and continue to needle felt firmly so it holds that position.

7. Legs. *Use either needle, and the dark fleece. Follow the steps below, or for a short-cut, try the wooden skewer technique on page 21.*

Split the fleece into four. Put one quarter aside for spare. Use two of the quarters to make the two longer fore-legs.

The remaining quarter can be split in two to make the two shorter back paws.

Roll each piece up tightly into a sausage shape, and needle felt along the length, turn over and repeat all around until approximately the size and length below.

8. Join the legs to the body. *Use the finer 38 gauge needle.*

One at a time, position both longer legs against the body, so they overhang at the bottom for the paw, like the drawing- right. Remember you can adjust the pose here, if you position the legs at the front, your fox will look forward, but if you move them around to the left or right, your fox will be looking off to the side, try it.

Needle felt the edge of each leg into the body all along the length, both sides to attach. Cover the top of the legs with some spare fox-coloured fleece and keep needling to blend them in.

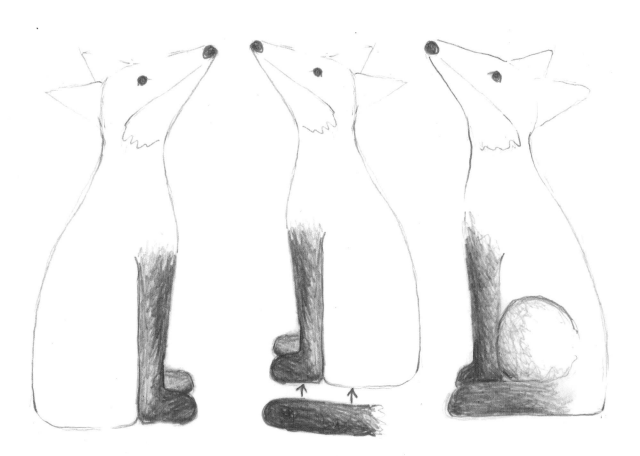

Sit the fox on the foam pad and bend the paws up and forward, and needle felt into the crease . Needle felt underneath and all around the fold to fix the paws in position.

Add the shorter back paws. Position them horizontally at each side of the base of the model (so that all four paws are in line) and one at a time needle felt into place with the finer, 38 gauge needle.

To create the back thigh, roll up some fox coloured fleece into a ball and needle felt into position above each back paw.

9. Tail.

Roll up some of the remaining fleece for the tail into a sausage shape, and needle felt along the length a little. Leave the base end loose for attaching to the body. Add some more fleece to plump up the middle of the tail, and add some white at the tip.

Position as you like on the the model and needle felt some fibres from the tail right into the body to secure.

Finishing touches.

Add some white fleece below the neck to create the chest.

Keep needle felting all over the fox to refine the shape and firm up the model, adding more fleece to build up areas .

Make a lovely woodland garland using real acorn cups.

Use a selection of your favourite colours of fleece.

Roll up small amounts of fleece into tight bundles and needle felt into acorn shapes.

You can make them quickly by adapting the bamboo skewer technique on page 21.

Make sure the fleece is rolled at the very tip of the skewer, so the shape is not too long.

Use a dab of pva glue or a hot glue gun to fix the felt acorns into the cups, and hot glue~gun them onto a string. If you prefer, you can drill two small holes into the acorn cups first and thread them onto a line before attaching the acorns.

Robin

Robin red~breast made with shetland moorit fleece and garden~wire legs. Height about 7 cm. A very simple egg shape makes up the body with the wings and tail attached.
For a more realistic look, the wire legs can be made with florist wire that is bound with brown paper, or you can wrap them with thread for a lifelike, wrinkly texture.

Robin

Materials you will need

8 grammes wool fleece, plus a little
spare
A little red and white fleece for details
Black fleece for beak see page 21 or 24
Wire robin legs, see page 25
2 small black 4mm beads for eyes

Size will be about 8 - 10cm
Time to needle felt 2 to 2 1/2 hours

tail

wings

1/2
body

spare

Robin 8 gms fleece
Try~shetland moorit
Dyed red/ orange
Shetland, or
Norwegian, or
Corriedale
White or grey shetland

1 Body.

Use the 36 gauge triangle needle.
*Split the 8 grammes of fleece in two, and put half
aside for making the wings and tail later...*
*Roll the other half of fleece tightly into a bundle
and hold firmly on top of the sponge.*
*Push the felting needle deeply into the bundle
and repeat until it holds together without
springing back open. Turn the bundle over and
continue to needle felt all around, until the wool
firms up and shrinks.*
*Aim roughly for the shape and size on the left.
Needle felt all around the bottom to make it nice
and rounded. You can add little of the spare
fleece to form the top of the head if necessary.*

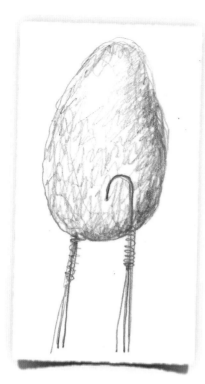

2. Join the legs to the body.

Use the fine 38 gauge star needle and take your time as you may catch the wire loop, and snap the needle.

Split the remaining fleece in two and put half aside to make the wings and tail. Use some of the remaining spare fleece to attach the legs.

You are aiming to cover the loop of the leg and trap this under the fibres so it doesn't fall out.

Hold one wire leg in place at the base of the large end of the body. Lay some fleece over the top of the loop and needle felt into the body.

Add more fleece to cover the wire loop completely. You can also add a little underneath the leg to prevent wobbly legs.

Turn the body over and repeat with the other leg at the opposite side.

3. Beak. *To make the beak, see the instructions on page 21 or 24*

First try holding the beak in various positions against the head to see which direction looks good.

Using the finer 38 gauge star needle, hold the beak in place and push the needle in quite deeply all around the edge catching some fibres from the beak and pushing them into the head.

You will need to add some small wisps of red fibre over the edge, above , below and all the way around, to secure the beak.

4. Red Breast.

Continue to add small tufts of red fleece to create the red breast of the robin.

Add some white or grey fleece in a crescent at the base of the red .

5. Eyes.

Use the felting needles to pin the beads into a position you like on the head.

1. Knot a double thread and sew into the position of one eye through to the other side.

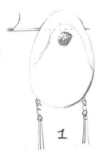

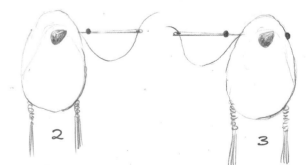

2. Attach the first bead and sew back through in the other direction to the original stitch.

3. Attach the second bead and stitch right through the head again. You can repeat the stitches to make the eyes secure, then cut the thread close to the surface.

Using the finer needle, place a tiny wisp of white fibre over each bead, and gently push the needle in deeply, all around the edge of each bead to create a highlight.

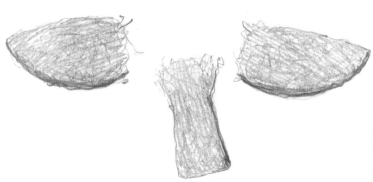

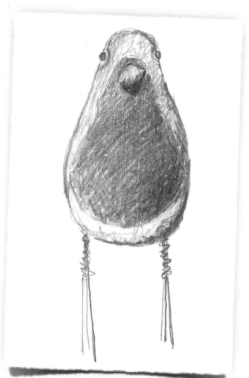

6. Wings. *Use either needle.*

With the remaining fleece put aside, split this in two, and put half aside for the tail. Use the other half for making the wings. Fold them into a loose wing shape, and try them for size. Adjust the amount of fleece if necessary.

One at a time, needle felt the fleece flat onto the sponge. Peel from the surface, turn over and repeat until the wing flattens more, then you can needle inwards to shape them. See page 23 for some tips on shaping.

Leave the edge to be joined to the body a little loose.

Position each wing against the body, trying different positions.

One at a time needle felt the wing to the body.

7. Tail. *Use some of the remaining fleece to make a tail.*

Roll up a little into a wedge shape, and try it for size, and adjust if necessary. Use the same technique as for the wings. Position onto the robin and needle felt into place.

Finishing touches.

Continue to needle felt all over the robin to give a smooth surface. Add more fleece if it needs plumping up.

When you are happy with the result, carefully open out the wire toes and bend at right angles. Bend three toes out to the front and one toe at the back of each foot.

Make a few adjustments so that he stands without wobbling.

To make some snails to go with your robin, collect and wash some empty real shells, and make the needle felted body like the drawings on page 72. Glue body into the shell with some pva or hot glue gun.

Badger

Badger made with masham, and black and white fleece. Length (standing)
about 10 to 12 cm.
Make this lovely striped character, then make his family too.
To make cubs, use less fleece, to make them smaller, but increase the size of
the head and eyes, and pose in playful positions.

Badger

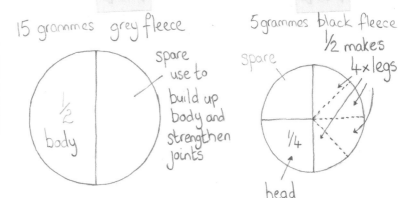

15 grammes grey fleece

½ body

spare use to build up body and strengthen joints

5 grammes black fleece

½ makes 4 x legs

spare

¼

head

Materials you will need

15 grammes grey wool fleece for body.
5 grammes black for head and legs.
White fleece for stripes.
Wire for inside legs (optional)
2 small black 3mm beads for eyes.

Size will be about 10 to 12 cm
Time to needle felt 3 to 4 hours.

Badger~ 15 grammes grey –
masham, Jacob, or
Shetland,
5 grammes black dyed
Shetland, Norwegian pels.
White cheviot, or
shetland

1 Body.

Use the 36 gauge triangle needle
Split the 15 grammes of fleece in two, and
put half aside for spare and tail.
Roll the other half of fleece tightly into an
oblong bundle and hold firmly on top of the
sponge.
Push the felting needle deeply into the
bundle and repeat until it holds together
without springing back open. Turn the
bundle over at intervals and continue
needle felting so the wool firms up and
shrinks.
Aim roughly for the shape and size on the
left.
Leave the neck end slightly loose for
attaching a head.
Needle felt all around the tail end to make it
rounded. You can add more of the spare
fleece later to build up the badger.

2. Head.

Use the finer 38 gauge star needle and the black fleece.

Split the 5 grammes of black fleece in two and put half aside for the four legs.

Split the remainder in two again, putting half aside for spare.

The remaining amount should be just right to make the head. Roll this up into a smaller, tight bundle and try it for size against the body. Adjust the amount of fleece if necessary. Needle felt to create a pointed cone shape, as above left. You can pull out the nose a little, and needle felt all along the length. Turn the head over occasionally, and continue to felt all around the head until firm.

For the lovely striped face, pull some small, thin amounts of fibre from the white fleece and position along the top of the length of the head. Attach with shallow jabs from the finer needle. Repeat this along each side of the head to create the stripes and add a little more to create the cheeks.

3. Nose. *Use the finer 38 gauge star needle.*

Roll up a very small amount of black fleece into a bobble in your fingers and palms and needle felt this into the tip of the nose.

4. Ears. *Use the finer 38 gauge needle, and shallow jabs onto the foam, this will be quite fiddly!*

Take two small 'tufts' of white fleece, and one at a time, roll up loosely in your fingers and palms into a ball. Try them for size against the head, and adjust the amount of fleece if necessary. Needle felt each flat on top of the sponge, peel off, turn over and needle to flatten the other side.

Needle felt around the edges towards the centre to make the ears round.

Add a few tiny wisps of black fibre to the centre of the ears, and needle felt this in place.

Position each ear at the end of the black stripes on the head as above. Attach to the head by pushing some fibres from the ear deep into the head with steady, deep jabs. Blend over the join with some of the spare black fleece.

5. Eyes.

Use the felting needles to carefully pin the beads onto the head. Try different positions on the face, until you like the way it looks.

Sew the eyes in place following the guide on page 31.

6. Join the head to the body. *Use the finer, 38 gauge star needle.*
Position the head onto the body, try different positions to create the pose. Hold in place firmly on top of the foam pad, and needle felt the loose fibres from the neck of the body into the back of the head, and some under the chin.
Be careful not to stab through into your fingers!
Turn the model over and repeat all the way around. Add some more spare grey fleece to build up the neck and help to secure the head to the body.
Keep needling to firm up and shape the neck, adjust the angle of the head if needed, and felt it firmly in position.

7. Legs. *Use either needle and the black fleece put aside for the legs, split into four. Try the wooden skewer technique on page 21. If you wish to add wire for support in the legs, roll up each length, (about 2.5cm) inside the fleece.*
Roll one piece up tightly into a sausage shape. Try for size against the body, and adjust the amount of fleece for each leg if necessary. Needle felt all four legs until firm, leaving the top end a little loose for attaching to the body. Needle felt the bottom end into a paw shape.

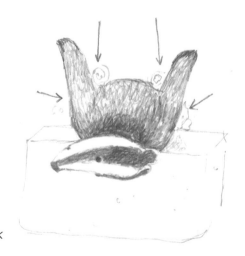

8. Join the legs to the body.
Use the finer 38 gauge star needle,
One at a time, position each leg against the body. Needle felt the top of each leg into the body. Secure the joints by adding some spare 'tufts' of grey fleece over the top and underneath the joint.
You can adjust the position or stride of the legs, and check the length, then needle felt some more to firm up the joint.

Finishing touches...
Roll up a small amount of grey fleece for a tail and needle felt into a short sausage shape, loose at one end, then attach to the body.
Keep needle felting all over the badger to refine the shape and firm up the model, adding more fleece to build up areas if necessary.

To make some woodland toadstools, roll up some fleece for the stalk, leave the top loose for attaching to the cap. Make the top nice and domed and add some colourful spots or pattern.

83

To make some butterflies, or dragonflies, roll up a small amount of fleece for the body. Make the wings flat, decorate, and attach to the body. Use pins or wire to make the antenna.

Unicorn

Little white unicorn made with cheviot fleece, height about 10 cm
The unicorn can be posed in so many elegant ways so make a pair, or family.
You can easily change the unicorn into a Pegasus by swapping the horn for a
little pair of wings on his back.

Unicorn

Materials you will need
10 grammes white wool fleece.
Plus some spare
Wire and thread unicorn horn see page 24
Wire lengths for inside the legs about 3 to 4 cm
2 small black 2mm beads for eyes

Size will be about 8 - 10cm
Time to needle felt 3 hours

10 grammes white fleece

head including 1/4 of this for 2 ears

neck

1/2 body

1/4

4 x legs

unicorn~ 10 gms white fleece Jacob, cheviot, white-faced woodland, Dorset horn, Suffolk.

1 Body.
Use the 36 gauge triangle needle.
Split the 10 grammes of fleece in two, and put half aside for making the head and legs later...
Roll the other half of fleece tightly into a bundle and hold firmly on top of the sponge.
Push the felting needle deeply into the bundle and repeat until it holds together without springing back open. Turn the bundle over and continue to needle felt all around.
Aim roughly for the shape and size on the left.
Leave the neck end slightly loose for attaching the neck and head.
Needle felt all around the tail end to make it nice and rounded.
Later you can add more fleece if desired.

2. Head.

Use the finer 38 gauge star needle. This will be a bit fiddly.

Take a look at the diagram showing the amounts of fleece to use, it will help with the next stage.

Split the remaining fleece in two, and put half aside for the four legs. Split the remainder in two again, putting half aside for the neck. (It may help to label these amounts, to save confusion)

The remaining amount should be just right for making the head, including the ears, so take about a quarter away for making two ears and put this to the side for now...

Have a look at the diagram above, half of the amount left for the head (now quite small) is wrapped around the wire loop and needle felted into a bundle all around and through the loop, to secure the unicorn horn. You should use the finer needle to do this part and push the needle in slowly so it doesn't snap against the wire.

When you have secured the wire loop inside, you can add the other half of remaining fleece for the nose and shape the whole head.

Roll it up into a little bundle and position at the front of the head to create the nose, push the needle through the nose part and aim into the back part to join the fibres together.

Continue to needle felt along the length of the nose and head until firm and small. The head should shrink to about the size drawn above, if it is still large and squashy, keep going, or if it is a bit small, add some spare fleece.

3. Ears.

Use the finer 38 gauge star needle, and the pointed tip of a moistened wooden skewer, this will also be quite fiddly!

Take the small amount of the fleece put aside for the ears and split in two.

Wrap each tiny piece of fibre around the very tip of the skewer. Twist the skewer whilst pinching the fibre until it tightens around the tip, forming a tight bundle.

Pull the pointed bundle off, and push the needle through so the fibres don't unravel.

Try them for size, if the ears seem too big, make two more, using less fibre for each, from the spare fleece.

Position at the back of the head at an angle you like, and attach to the head one at a time by pushing some fibres from the base of the ear into the head.

4. Eyes.

Use the felting needles to pin the beads onto the head, try different places until you like the way it looks.

Sew the beads onto the head as described on page 34.

5. Neck.

Take half of the fleece put aside for the neck, roll up into a sausage shape, and needle felt a little. Resting on top of the foam, position the neck against the body, and attach by directing the needle and pushing some the fibre from the neck into the body. Turn over and needle from the other side, and all around the join until the neck is blended to the body. Use more spare fleece to blend in the join.

Leave the top end loose for attaching the head.

6. Join the head to the neck. *Use the finer, 38 gauge star needle.*

Position the head against the neck and hold firmly on top of the sponge.

Needle felt some fibres from the neck into the head, turn over and repeat all the way around to secure the join. Be careful not to push the needle through into your fingers!

Keep needling to firm up and shape the neck, adding more spare fibre if needed. You can adjust the angle the head is facing slightly to create a pose, and needle this firmly so it holds the position.

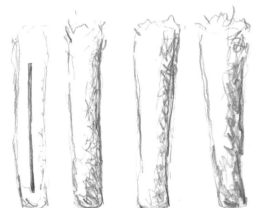

7. Legs. *Use 38 gauge star, and the fleece put aside for the legs, follow the steps below, or try the bamboo skewer technique on page 21.*

Split the fleece into four. The short lengths of wire are going to be trapped inside, so use the finer needle and avoid hitting the wire if you can.

One at a time, place the wire on top of each piece of fleece and roll each piece up tight into a sausage shape, and needle felt all along the length, and all around until firm.

Leave the top end loose for attaching to the body.

Aim for the size and length above left, and check them for size against the body.

Needle felt directly into the bottom end to form a hoof.

One at a time, position each leg against the body, using the finer needle, needle felt the top of each leg into the body.

Secure the joints by adding some spare fleece over, and under the joint.

You can adjust the position/ stride of the legs, then needle felt some more to firm up the joint.

Finishing touches. *Use the 38 gauge star needle.*
Roll up a small amount of fleece for a tail and needle felt loosely into a long sausage shape, leave loose at the tip. Position and attach to the body.
Using the coarse, hair-like fibre, pinch a small amount in your fingers, fold the length in half and needle felt the folded part into the back of the neck. Repeat this in a line to form the mane, then trim the length with scissors.
Keep needling all over the unicorn to refine the shape and firm up, adding more fleece to build up if desired.

89

Seahorse

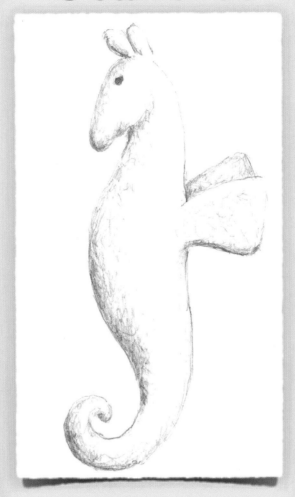

Seahorse made from the tail up. Height
about 11 to 12 cm.
Inside the tail is a length of wire, which is
coiled around to make the spiral shape.
Enjoy decorating these with colourful
patterns or sparkly beads or sequins

Seahorse

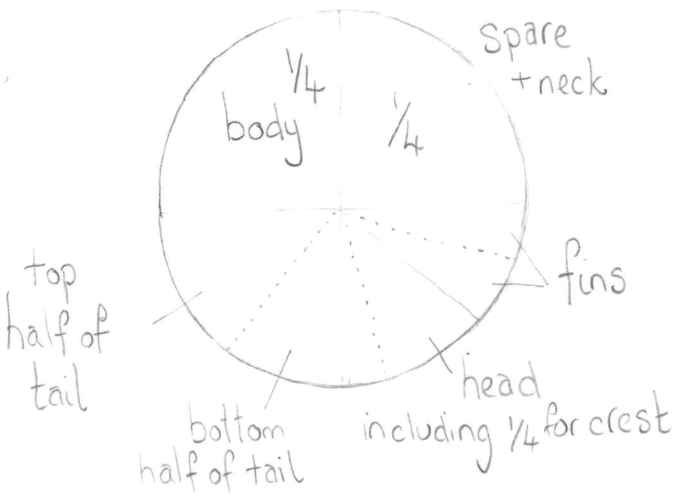

The circular guide diagram labels:
- 1/4 body
- 1/4
- Spare + neck
- top half of tail
- fins
- bottom half of tail
- head including 1/4 for crest

Materials you will need

6 grammes wool fleece, colour of your choice

Some coloured shades for decoration or beads or sequins for sparkle

2 small black 2mm beads for eyes

Wire length (about 6 cm) for curling the tail

Size will be about 8 - 10cm

Time to needle felt 2- 3 hours

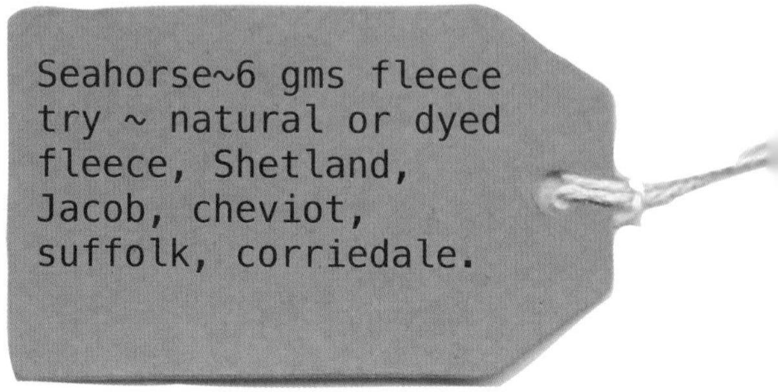

Seahorse~6 gms fleece
try ~ natural or dyed
fleece, Shetland,
Jacob, cheviot,
suffolk, corriedale.

1. Tail.

Use the finer 38 gauge star needle and the straight length of wire to form the tail. Later you can bend the tail into a spiral.

Follow the guide and needle felt as below or try the wooden skewer technique on page 21.

Split the 6 grammes of fleece in two, and put half aside for making the rest of the seahorse later...split the remaining half in two again, and put half aside for the belly.

Split the remainder in two one more time, put half aside for making the top of the tail.

Make the long thin tail with the remainder.

Place the straight piece of wire onto the fleece and roll up tightly into a sausage shape and hold firmly on top of the sponge.

Needle felt all along the length, turn over and repeat all around until the fleece firms up and shrinks to about the size on the left.

Leave the top end loose.

Carefully push the wire back into the tail if it moves, and continue to needle felt.

If wire shows through, cover up with a few more fibres.

Avoid hitting the wire by lowering the angle of the needle to more horizontal.

Use the other half of fleece put aside for
the tail to extend the tail upwards. Roll
into a bundle and hold on top of the
sponge and needle felt the fibres together
to form the shape to the right, below.
Leave the top a little loose for joining to
the body.

2. Body

Use either needle, and the fleece put aside for the
body.

Roll the fleece up tightly into a bundle and needle felt
into an oval shape. Position the body above the tail you
have made and hold on top of the sponge. Needle felt
the fibres from the tail into the body to join the two
together. Add some fleece from the spare to blend in
the join if needed. See picture on the right, centre.
Using some pointed pliers pinch the end of the tail with
the wire inside and bend the tail into a coil as on the
right.

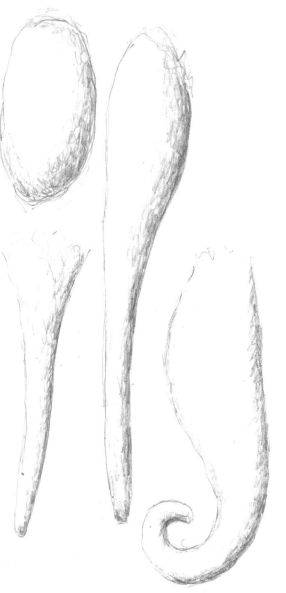

3. Head. Use the 38 gauge star needle.

Split the remaining fleece in two and put half aside for
neck and some spare.
Split the remainder in two again, putting half aside for
the two fins or wings.
The remainder should be just right for the head,
including the little fan or ears on top, so take away
about a quarter for these.
Roll the remainder up tightly into a bundle to form the
head.
Try this for size onto the body, and adjust the amount of
fleece if necessary.
Needle felt all around until firm and just right for the
head, about the size above.

4. Ears or crest.

Roll up tiny pieces of fibre in your
fingers and palms, or try the
wooden skewer technique on
page 21
Make 2 or 3 little bobbles and
attach to the head with the finer
38 gauge needle.

5. Eyes.

Use the felting needles to pin the beads onto the head. Try different positions until you like the way it looks.

Sew the beads into the head in the same way described on page 31.

6. Join the head to the body.

Use the finer, 38 gauge star needle.

Take a little of the spare fleece and needle felt into the top of the body to form a neck. Leave a little loose for attaching the head.

Position the head against the neck and hold firmly on top of the sponge.

Needle felt some fibres from the neck into the head, turn over and repeat all the way around to secure the join. Be careful not to push the needle through into your fingers!

Keep needling to firm up and shape the neck, adding more spare fleece if needed. You can adjust the angle the head is facing slightly to create a pose, and needle this firmly so it holds that position.

7. Fins. *Use either needle*

With the remaining fleece put aside for the fins, split this in two.

One at a time, needle felt the fleece flat onto the sponge. Peel from the surface, turn over and repeat until the wool flattens more, then needle felt inwards to shape the edges. See page 23 for some tips on shaping.

Leave the edge to be joined to the body a little loose.

Try different positions on the body, until you like the pose.

One at a time needle felt each fin onto to the body until secure.

Finishing touches

Continue to needle felt all over the seahorse to firm up and smooth the surface. Create a pattern with coloured fibres or add some sparkle by sewing on beads and sequins.

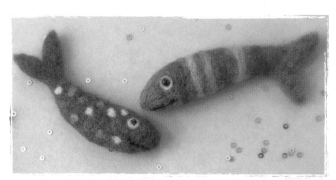

* Make a colourful shoal of fish. Roll up an oval/sausage shape and needle felt to make the body . Make the tail by twisting some fleece around the tip of a bamboo skewer to make two points, and attach to the body.
Decorate with coloured fibre, or beads and sequins for sparkle

Hare

Brown hare made with shetland moorit fleece
height about 10 to 12 cm.
Nice large ears make this model into a hare,
but if you wish to make a rabbit, make the ears
much smaller, and plump up the body more.
Make a group and change the colour of the
fleece to white, or a natural grey for variety.

Hare

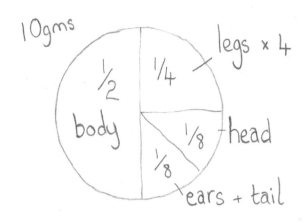

10gms

½ body

¼ legs x 4

⅛ head

⅛ ears + tail

Materials you will need

10 grammes wool fleece, plus some spare.
White fleece for details
2 small black 4mm beads for eyes
Whiskers- white masham or grey herdwick

Size will be about 8 - 10cm
Time to needle felt 3 to 4 hours

Hare~ 10gms fleece
Shetland moorit
Grey Shetland
White cheviot
Or Suffolk

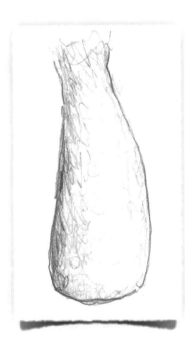

1. Body.
Use the 36 gauge triangle needle.
Split the 10 grammes of fleece in two, and put half aside for making the head and legs later...
Roll the other half of fleece tightly into a bundle and hold firmly on top of the sponge.
Push the felting needle deeply into the bundle and repeat until it holds together without springing back open. Turn the bundle over at intervals, and continue to needle felt all around.
Aim roughly for the shape and size on the left.
Leave the neck end slightly loose for attaching the head.
Needle felt directly into the bottom end to make it nice and flat.
Later you can add more spare fleece to build up the hare.

2. Head. *Use the 38 gauge star needle.*
Use the fleece put to one side and split in two, put half aside for the legs.
Split the remainder in two again, putting half to one side for the ears and tail.
The remaining amount should be just right for making the head. Roll it up as tight as you can and check it for scale against the body you have made. If it seems too large, just take away a bit of the fleece. If too small, add a little more from the spare. Needle felt this bundle all around . Felt a little more at one end to make it smaller and firm for the nose.

3. Ears. *Use either needle.*
With the fleece put aside for ears and tail, split in two, and put half aside for the tail. The other half should be just right for making two ears, split in two. Loosely roll each half between your palms into a long shape that when flattened down will make an ear. Try them for size against the head, if they seem too big and thick, make them with less fleece.
Needle felt them flat onto the sponge, peel off and turn over, and needle felt the other side, repeat until they are nice and flat and even.
Push the fibres on the outside of the ear into the centre to shape the edges and tip. See more details on shaping edges on page 23. Leave the fibres loose at the base of each ear for attaching to the head.
Position the ears against the back of the head, try different angles to create the pose. You can even fold the ear along the length to make a crease.
Join the ears to the head . One at a time, needle felt the loose fibres at the base, right into the head to secure them in place.

4. Eyes and nose..
Use the felting needles to pin the beads onto the head for the best position.
Sew the beads in place following the guide on page 31
Create the nose with a few more stitches to make the letter Y ~see more instructions on page 32
The whiskers are best applied as a finishing touch, or they will become crushed.

5. Join the head to the body. *Use the finer, 38 gauge needle.*

Position the head onto the body, try the head at different angles to create the pose. Hold in place firmly on the sponge and needle felt the loose fibres from the neck into head. Be careful not to stab through into your fingers!

Turn the model over and repeat all the way around. Add some more fleece to build up the neck and help to secure the head to the body.

Adjust the angle of the head if necessary, and needle felt some more to hold the position firm.

6. Legs. *Use either needle. Needle felt as below, or try a shortcut ~making them with the skewer technique on page 21*

Using the fleece put aside for the legs, split in two. Put one half aside for the back legs. Split the remaining half in two again for the two, longer fore~legs.

Roll each piece up tightly into a sausage shape, and needle along the length, turn over and repeat all around until approximately the size and length below.

Make the back paws. Split the fleece put aside for the back legs in two and put half aside for the thighs. Split the remaining amount in two and make the shorter back paws as drawn below, left.

7. Join the legs to the body.
Use the finer 38 gauge needle.
One at a time, position both longer legs against the body, so they overhang at the bottom for the paw, like the picture right.

Remember you can adjust the pose here, if you position the legs at the front, your hare will look forward, but if you move them around to the left or right, your hare will be looking off to the side, try it.

Needle felt the very edge of each leg into the body all along the length each side to attach. You can cover the top of the legs with some spare fleece to blend into the chest.

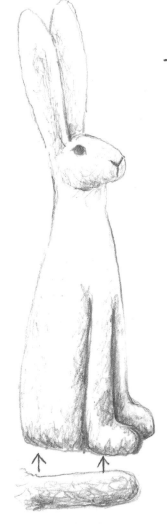

Sit the hare firmly on top of the sponge so that the paws bend up and forward, and needle felt into the crease . Needle felt underneath and all around the fold to fix the paws in position.

8. Add the back paws.

Position the shorter back paws horizontally at each side of the base of the model (so that all four paws are in line) and one at a time, needle felt into place with the finer 38 gauge needle.

To create the back thigh/haunch split the fleece put aside in two, roll up each into a ball and needle felt into position above each back paw.

9. Tail.

Roll up some of the remaining fleece for the tail into a small tight bundle, and try for size against the body. Needle felt it a little, hold in place on top of the sponge, and needle felt through the tail, into the body to attach.

10. Whiskers...

Use the fine 38 gauge needle and some coarse fibre, add as little or as much whisker as you like.
Pinch a tiny wisp of the hair~like fibre and fold in two.
Hold the folded end of fibre just over one side of the nose and slowly push some fibres deep into the nose with the needle. Repeat the other side and trim with scissors if desired. See more details on applying whiskers on page 35.

Finishing touches...

Use the fine 38 gauge needle. Build up the cheeks by adding small amounts of fleece to either side of the face. Add some fine white fleece to create the fluffy chest.
Add some very small wisps of fleece inside the ears, but keep the angle of the needle shallow or the white fibres will show through at the back of the ear.
Keep needle felting all over the hare to refine the shape and firm up the model, adding more fleece to build up areas if you wish.

To make the catkins, take some grey fleece and twist small amounts around the point of a wooden skewer to form little tight bundles. Add a tiny patch of brown fleece, and glue onto a twig-stem with a hot glue gun.

What next?   Be inspired!

I hope you are really happy with your needle felted creations, and have found it very rewarding seeing the characters emerge in your own hands.

Here are a few suggestions for what to do next, find inspiration, and develop your own style of needle felting. This will happen naturally or you can choose to work in a certain way, perhaps exaggerating certain elements of your models, or using specific colours or shades.

Create a portrait.

Work from photographs or real life to create a more lifelike portrait. Have plenty of different angles showing the front, back and profile. Look at the individual shapes that will make up the portrait, make them individually, then look at the angles and shapes as you join them together.

Collect inspiration

If you haven't done so already, treat yourself to a lovely sketchbook, and pens you like to use. Keep it handy when you are making, as ideas will come to you. Jot them down, draw or doodle them, record them for future ideas, before you know it, you are designing!

Or it can simply be a list to explore later, things that interest you, or that you have seen on your travels, or something you always wanted to make or collect.

Go large....think about the scale and size you would like to create.

To make the models larger, increase the amount of fleece to begin with.

If you wish to make much larger creations, you could build up a core to make the bulk of the model, then needle felt the surface. For example, try using coarse wool, sponge, pillow stuffing , polystyrene, or scraps of felt over a wire armature.

Experiment using an armature, just like a wire skeleton inside your model, making your character posable when complete. This will support the figure if it is large, complicated, or standing on one or two feet. Make the wire structure, then wrap fleece around the whole frame, needle felting as you go.

*Try different fibres. Make samples from them and keep notes of how they felted ,if you liked the feel, did they felt quick or slow. What would they be good for making? Different fibres or colours may give you ideas for future projects.

Enjoy your new skill with others, perhaps get a group of friends together, show them how to needle felt and share ideas.

If you know someone who would love to try needle felting, but maybe they do not have the confidence, or for a younger artist perhaps, try this quick, simple project~

Use a template.

From your kitchen, or cook shop, find some pastry or cookie cutters.

Place the fleece inside the cutter and needle felt inside. Turn over and repeat until the shape is formed.

This method is a simple way to quickly and safely create something to decorate, with little fingers protected outside the cutter.

Make a gift

This is a nice idea, make a keepsake for someone you know, what would it be, what would they like?

Before you know it you could be making a whole selection of lovely handmade gifts.

Troubleshooting

Needles breaking / bending ...
Try slowing down, keep the needle straight, and avoid putting sideways pressure on the needle. If there is some wire inside the wool, also slow down, and angle the needle to avoid hitting the wire.

Stabbing fingers... Take a break. Slow down. Make sure you are resting the model on top of the sponge, so the needle goes into the sponge and not you.
If this keeps happening, try protecting your fingers with fabric plasters.

Soft centre... When building up shapes, make sure your needle goes into the wool bundle deep enough to felt right through, and not just the surface.

Loose beak on robin or chicken... Try overlapping some tiny wisps of fibre over the edge of the beak where it joins the head, push the fibres right through the edge of the beak and into the head.

Wobbly head or legs... Try adding more fleece around or over the join and needle felt into place to firm up the connection.

Head too big... If the head is still soft, you can continue to needle felt and it will shrink a little more. Or try building up the body to match the scale of the head.
Or if nothing else works, take drastic action~remove the head (use sharp scissors) and make a new one, using less fleece!

Head too small... Add more fleece to enlarge the head.

Ears Too big... Before joining to the head, you could trim a little right at the base but make sure to cover the cut ends with a little fibre when you join the ear to the head.

Ears too small... Try gently pulling to stretch the felt bigger. Add some fibre to the outside edge to enlarge. Or simply make another ear, using slightly more fleece.

White detail shows through at back of ear... When adding the white detail to the inside of the ears, try not to needle felt too deeply, the fibres will come out the other side, so lower the needle to a more horizontal position. See page 22

Hard edge to a coloured or shaded patch... Soften the edge by blending like paint. Try mixing a small amount of both colours together with the carders and apply some small wisps along the edge of the coloured /shaded patch to soften the join. See page 15 for tips on carding.

Unstable and keeps falling over... The bottom of the model may be curved, and keep toppling over. Turn it upside down and try making the bottom of the model as flat and wide as you can. Add a little fleece all around the very edge of the bottom and needle felt any bulge in the centre to make it level.

Falling over ~chicken or robin... Adjust the wire toes, open them out as far as you can for stability, and adjust the angle of the legs. If this doesn't work, it may be due to the balance of weight, try adding some fleece to the front or back to even this out.

Lumps, bumps or creases... If the surface has creases, or lumps, just take some fine wisps of fleece to cover the uneven surface and gently needle felt into place with shallow jabs of the 38 gauge star needle.

Fuzzy surface... Keep needle felting all over with shallow jabs of the fine needle. If you still have some stray fuzzy fibres, trim all over with a small pair of scissors.

Pin holes... Little holes can remain in the surface of the wool, especially if it is a finer fibre. Try using the finer needle to gently needle felt, with shallow jabs all over the surface. Or gently brush the surface with the tip of a pin to stroke them away.

Wire end of leg shows through the felt... Try snipping back the wire as close into the surface as possible, and cover with a tiny wisp of fleece.
If a wire loop shows through, cover this with some more fleece and needle felt into place.

Suppliers

Felting Needles and Wool Fleece

Here are some UK suppliers of wool fleece for spinning, dying and felt making.

www.worldofwool.co.uk

www.wheeldalewoolcrafts.co.uk

www.winghamwoolwork.co.uk

www.adelaidewalker.co.uk

www.norwegianwool.co.uk

Sponge/foam

This can be ordinary car wash sponge, or bath sponge or upholstery foam

Available from homeware stores, fabric stores etc.

There are also flat brush pads available from the wool fleece suppliers above.

www.wilko.com

www.abakhan.co.uk

Wire

Garden wire from garden centres, ironmongers or homeware stores

Or try florist or jewellery wire from craft suppliers.

www.wilko.com

www.abakhan.co.uk

Beads

Different size beads are available from craft stores and jewellery findings suppliers.

www.abakhan.co.uk

ww.hobbycraft.co.uk

Other useful sites

www.feltmakers.com   The International Feltmakers Association

www.campaignforwool.com

Top row ~ portrait commissions. Middle row ~ handmade felt mermaid dresses, miniature gloves and hare~doll. Bottom row ~ hare puppet, wax model illustrated book characters 'Tiddly Tides', ceramic and handmade felt sculpture.

Jenny Barnett

Before discovering felt making, I worked for many years as a clay modeller, sculpting for giftware companies like Coalport, Wedgwood, Genesis Fine Arts, and designing collectible figurines under the name of Jenny Oliver's faeries.

From then I went on to create a range of expressive sculpture of mothers and children, combining the fired ceramic figures with handmade felt.

These have gradually transformed into dolls and animal characters, and the clay has been replaced with wool fleece.

Now there is a growing collection of needle felted animal sculpture, handmade dolls, miniature felt garments, portrait commissions, illustration of my husband's story books, postcards, needle felting kits and workshops, and books.

I am adding creations to the range, and new developments can be seen on the following web pages.

Please get in touch if you would like to know more.

jennyneedlefelt@gmail.com

www.jennybarnett.co.uk
www.jenny-barnett.blogspot.co.uk
www.facebook.com/jennybarnettfelt

Left to right~ ceramic, felt and fabric sculpture, ceramic doll heads, handmade felt dress with vintage lace.